Anonymous

Scenes in the West

The Sunday-School and Temperance

Anonymous

Scenes in the West
The Sunday-School and Temperance

ISBN/EAN: 9783743394414

Manufactured in Europe, USA, Canada, Australia, Japa

Cover: Foto ©Lupo / pixelio.de

Manufactured and distributed by brebook publishing software (www.brebook.com)

Anonymous

Scenes in the West

SCENES IN THE WEST,

OR

The Sunday-School

AND

TEMPERANCE.

BY A MISSIONARY.

PHILADELPHIA:
LUTHERAN BOARD OF PUBLICATION,
42 NORTH NINTH STREET.
1873.

PREFACE.

THE author of this volume has brought together a few incidents in *real* life to illustrate the power of godliness in the individual, and the blessings of the Sunday-school, the influence of the prayer-meeting and the cause of temperance in the church and in the community.

That the God of all our mercies may bless this little book to the reader, is the prayer of the author.

CHAPTER.		PAGE.
I.	The Missionary	13
II.	Misfortunes	27
III.	Relief Obtained	39
IV.	An Appointment	45
V.	The Missionary Preaches	56
VI.	Mr. Steele's Meeting	62
VII.	Mr. Mason and Mr. Wilson	69
VIII.	Missionary Visits	78
IX.	Opposition	84
X.	Sunday-school Organized—Local Preacher	92
XI.	Mr. Kerr and his Family	98
XII.	The Temperance Cause	109
XIII.	Mr. Truman—Missionary's Departure	118

CHAPTER.		PAGE.
XIV.	Workings of the Sunday-school and Temperance Society	123
XV.	George and Mary	134
XVI.	Mr. Brown's Family	140
XVII.	Missionary Again Visits the West	145
XVIII.	Death	152

SCENES IN THE WEST.

CHAPTER I.

THE MISSIONARY.

"The melancholy days had come,
The saddest of the year."

ALL nature seemed to be resting in a quiet dreamy slumber. The bee had well nigh laid up its winter store, and many of the birds were preparing to leave for more genial climes in the sunny south. All these were but the harbingers of the cold storms that were lingering behind the snow-covered mountains of the north. Indian summer, the season of romance, like the life of a humble Christian, leaves its loveliest scenes to its departing hours. It was in the midst of these balmy days that you might have seen a traveler with a worn satchel in one hand and a staff in the other coming up a narrow lane leading to the home of a prosperous Western settler. He walked slowly, for he had left behind him many weary miles; his countenance, though calm, was pale and languid; yet his eye seemed to bespeak the hope that here he might find the much-needed rest.

Two men were standing beside the gate at the end of the lane when the stranger came up. The one was a kindly disposed person with but little force of character, and deficient in moral courage, whom we shall know as Mr. Kerr. The other, whose name was Steele, was the owner of the premises.

He was a large man, selfish and resolute, a conceited formalist, bigoted, exceedingly headstrong, and greatly prejudiced against all Christian zeal.

No sooner did Mr. Steele notice the approach of the stranger than he turned to Mr. Kerr and exclaimed: "There, I'll bet you, comes that Sunday-school, temperance loafer I've heard so much of lately. I reckon he expects to get in here; but I tell you, sir, my 'shanty' don't hold the like of him, while I'm boss here, 'that's said!'" This was uttered with emphatic bitterness. To this passionate outburst Mr. Kerr ventured a little palliation by the remark that he had heard that in the other settlement the people seemed to like the missionary very well.

"*You* would have nothing to do with his nonsense, would you?" retorted Mr. Steele with a look of scorn.

No," feebly and insincerely muttered Mr. Kerr, "we have got along so far without it, and I guess we can get along without it a little further."

"That's my ticket," sharply added Mr. Steele.

By this time the stranger had reached the gate. A calm, pleasant smile lit up his pale countenance; and he accosted them with,

"Good evening, friends."

"Good evening, sir," responded Mr. Kerr.

"How d'ye do, sir," thundered out Mr. Steele.

"This has been a very pleasant day," ventured the traveler.

"Yes, sir," curtly replied Mr. Steele.

"I am very tired," continued the stranger; "could I stay with you to-night?"

"You are the fellow who goes about lecturing on temperance, and getting up Sunday-schools, aint you?" sarcastically rejoined Mr. Steele, his face reddening.

"That is my calling," meekly added the man of God.

"Then you don't stay all night in my house; I don't harbor fellows who are too lazy to work," sneeringly answered the excited Mr. Steele.

"But I am very tired, and my head aches badly; I'll pay you well."

"Cant help it. The sooner you make tracks the better," retorted the unfeeling man.

"I am afraid it will storm to-night," continued the missionary, pointing to a dark cloud which was looming up in the west.

"You might have stayed at home and minded your own business, instead of minding other people's, and kept out of this trouble," replied Mr. Steele, with a look so severe that the poor wanderer lost all hope of any comfort or favor from this seemingly inhospitable dwelling; so he inquired how far it was to the next house.

"That depends entirely upon which way you go," mockingly answered the hard-hearted man, with a wink to Mr. Kerr, and a conceited smile at the unfeeling wit he had displayed.

"I expect to continue my labors westward," gently added the missionary.

His soul was grieved at the hardness of this man's heart, and for a moment he felt like looking upon his persecutor with anger. But he remembered that even his Lord and Master was mocked and derided; that "when He was reviled, He reviled not again; but as a lamb before his shearers is dumb, so He opened not his mouth." And the humble follower of the Man of Sorrows in silence offered up the prayer, "Father, forgive them, they know not what they do."

The door of common humanity being closed against him, he made up his mind to continue his journey, let the dangers and privations be what they might. An angel seemed to whisper, "I will lead thee in the way in which thou shalt go;" so he took courage.

Being thirsty, he ventured to ask for a drink of water.

"You can go to the spring," was the abrupt answer, and the cruel man turned upon his heel, and in company with Mr. Kerr passed on to the barn, leaving the suffering one standing by the gate alone.

But George, a lad of about ten years, and Mary, a little flower of seven summers, had looked on and listened with the curiosity common to children. Their hearts were filled with pity toward the poor man; and, when even a drink of water was denied him, the inherent kindness, implanted in all our natures, was instantly awakened.

In a moment, as the missionary turned the corner of the yard, the two children met him each with "a cup of cold water." "Here is good fresh water, please drink," said the little ones. His heart was melted at this unexpected exhibition of kindness; and invoking a blessing upon the dear children, he raised the cup to his lips and was refreshed. He then opened his satchel, and gave each child a picture card and Sunday-school paper, also cards for the men, together with a neat little tract for their mother. Bidding them good-by, he with a sigh resumed his lonely journey.

The children, happy in having done a kindness, hurried to their mother, and were soon showing and admiring the papers and cards; she, mother-like, very naturally shared their pleasure, but thought of the stranger with a pang of regret, for she feared that he would take the road leading into an unsettled region, infested with wild beasts and roving Indians. After admiring the pictures, she told the children all she knew of the Sunday-school, for which these beautiful things were made, at the same time hoping that her husband's opposition to them might be removed.

"I wish there was Sunday-school here," said George.

"Won't there be Sunday-school here, mother?" exclaimed both at once.

"I'm afraid not," said their mother, sorrowfully, knowing the hostility of many of the neighbors toward anything of the kind.

"Why not, mother?" innocently asked the children.

"This was one of those questions children often ask, and which it is so hard to answer.

"I don't know," she replied, evasively, adding, "go give your father and Mr. Kerr their cards. They are at the barn."

Hurrying out, their noisy delight soon arrested the attention of the men.

"What in the world is up now?" wondered their father.

"See here, father, see here!" exclaimed the children, holding out the cards.

"Who gave you these?" said he, reaching out his hand for the gifts, and suspecting the source.

"The man at the gate; we gave him a drink, and he gave us these (showing their cards) and a little book for mother, and this one for you and that one for Mr. Kerr."

Looking for a moment at the engraving, he read, "For I was an hungered, and ye gave me meat; I was thirsty, and ye gave me drink; I was a stranger, and ye took me in."

Instantly the terrible reproof, associated with these words, awakened the man's slumbering conscience. Writhing under its force he tried to construe the innocent gift into an insult; then flinging it to the ground he stamped his foot upon it.

At this exhibition of anger all the joy of the children vanished.

Mary began to cry, and George wondered what there was about the card to offend his father.

In the meantime, Mr. Kerr had read his card. The words were, "And *these* shall go away into everlasting punishment, but the righteous into life eternal."

"What have you got?" sneeringly asked Mr. Steele, of his companion. Mr. Kerr read the text with some emotion.

"Just what I expected! he thought to give

us a cut," said the angry man, at the same time adding many abusive words.

Mr. Kerr tried to assent to the remarks, but the words upon the card had touched his heart; and he felt like hating himself for having yielded, against his convictions, to the unreasonableness of his neighbor toward an unoffending stranger. Putting the card in his pocket, he was compelled to be an unwilling listener to the tirade of a would-be Christian (for Mr. Steele was a member of church) against prayer-meetings, temperance societies and Sunday-schools.

As soon as practicable, Mr. Kerr left for home; his conscience still at work, accusing him of cowardice, and partaking of another's sin. "And these shall go away into everlasting punishment," like a poisoned arrow was festering in his heart, until his guilty imagination conceived that the card contained his eternal doom.

Meeting his wife at the door of his house, he handed her the fatal card.

"Oh, the kind stranger gave you this!" she exclaimed with animation. "He was here this afternoon, and gave each of us one of the same kind, and left one for you. And then he prayed with us. I wish he would settle here and get up a Sunday-school, of which he talked so much. I believe he is one of the best of men."

"I wish so too;" involuntarily broke from the full heart of the stricken man; "I believe he is a good man. He came to Mr. Steele's a few hours ago, but was turned off."

"Why didn't you bring him home with you?" she asked.

"Well, I know I ought to have done so; but I was afraid of Mr. Steele, who you know hates all such people." To avoid any more questions on the subject, he asked to see what the man had left for him. The card was soon handed him, and he read: "Fear not them which kill the body, but are not able to kill the soul; but rather fear Him who is able to destroy both soul and body in Hell."

This was another arrow from the quiver of the Almighty. His wife soon detected the change that had come over him, and with becoming solicitude endeavored to find out the cause; but in this her efforts were evaded.

"I was afraid of Mr. Steele," thought he, "who would not even dare to kill my body—whilst I did not fear Him who is able to destroy my soul." Leaving him in his sorrow, we will return to Mr. Steele.

The children, mortified and discouraged, had left the barn, and gone to their mother for consolation in their disappointment. This was always afforded them; for never was a mother more kind to her little ones, and yet more decided in her endeavors to train them in the right way.

Mr. Steele, being conscious of having done wrong, tried to rid himself of his unpleasant feelings, by bustling about, doing first this, then that, for relief. It was late before he entered the house, and lest he should be suspected of regretting what he had done, he confronted his wife with, "I wonder what kind of trash that loafer left here with you and the children to-day? I guess he wants to set up an agency here."

"They are in the bureau drawer," there, said his wife, "shall I get them for you?"

"No, I don't want to see any more of the trash;" and, going into another room, he sat down to read a political speech. But it failed to interest him. The coming darkness, the looming up of heavy clouds in the distance, the stranger out in the pathless wilds, the abused privilege of doing good to—perhaps, after all—one of the followers of the Redeemer; the text on the card with its indirect reproof, were thoughts which crowded themselves upon his mind. For a moment he wished that he had given the stranger shelter; but prejudice had too long held sway to be thus easily set aside. He had taken a stand, and he would maintain it, let the consequences be what they would.

CHAPTER II.

MISFORTUNES.

OUR traveler, after leaving Mr. Steele's, unfortunately took a road leading from the inhabited portion of country. Night was approaching, and the last sounds of human habitations had long since ceased to greet his ear; he still walked on, however, hoping that some dwelling would come into view.

The sun had set behind the great mountain of storm clouds in the west, and twilight was drawing a curtain of darkness around. The clouds rose higher and higher; the heavens began to be overspread with long masses of floating vapor, and the distant gleam of lightning could now be distinctly seen. He now encountered a steep hill in his march; his limbs could scarcely bear his body along, but he knew that he must go on. There were but few trees on the hill, and their absence enabled him to see his way more clearly in ascending, but the valley beyond seemed shrouded in midnight darkness.

These wild regions were infested with wolves and other ravenous beasts, and our hero being unarmed, his life became hourly more endangered. After struggling along under accumulating difficulties, in utter loneliness and discouragement he sat down on a log to rest. It was to him an hour of trial; and his patience almost failed him. But the remembrance of God's promise, "Behold, I am with thee and will keep thee," cheered him. A clap of thunder warned him of the approach of the storm, and aroused his enfeebled energies to their task. But where should he go? The darkness, if possible, had increased; not a ray of light remained, excepting when the electric fluid for a moment lit up the heavens with its lurid blaze only to leave it still darker. An effort to secure shelter must be made *at once.*

As he was anxiously hurrying on among the weeds and fallen timber, a huge rattlesnake that had coiled itself under some rubbish suddenly sounded its "death-rattle." Finding that danger was threatening in the heavens above, and lurking on the earth beneath, he was on the point of sitting down and awaiting his fate, when, suddenly, a flash of lightning revealed an opening between the tall trees, and the hope that there might be some human habitation not far distant caused him to again renew his efforts.

Moving cautiously forward, he succeeded in crossing a stream of water; a short distance beyond was an old, broken-down fence. The glimpse which the lightning gave him of this, the work of man, sent a thrill of joy to his desponding heart.

He anxiously watched for the electric lamp to reveal the place of habitation. Now and then a large drop of rain fell, and presently a fearful blaze of lightning illuminated the whole heavens, followed by a clap of thunder that seemed to shake the earth to its very foundation! The rain was now descending upon the distant hill. Aroused to a full sense of his danger, he commended his soul to God, expecting to be crushed beneath the falling timber, which could plainly be heard above the roar of the elements.

As we all shrink from imminent danger, he instinctively looked around for some protection. Near by, in a clump of trees, he espied, when it again lightened, something like a roof. What a thrill of joy entered his heart! Groping his way forward, he found a little hut with door wide open as if to welcome him; he needed no invitation, but rushed in, for the storm was bursting upon him.

All within was dark and silent save a rustling in one corner and the flitting of a bat overhead. The chilly dampness which pervaded the room, and the musty smell that came up from the floor, made the first impression far from agreeable. The roof leaked and the windows were gone. In one corner he found a dry spot; here he nestled down, awaiting the fury of the descending storm.

The elements were now raging with irresistible power. The very earth seemed to tremble under the contending forces that were hurling destruction all around. Part of the shattered roof came down, the trees were torn up by the roots and the cabin was almost lifted from its foundation.

Happily the winds hurled the rain against the corner in which he had taken refuge, and the logs, chinking and daubing that remained, arrested the water, so that the place which he occupied was comparatively dry, whilst all the rest of the inside was deluged with the dashing rain.

Musing for a time upon his lonely condition and his prospects for the future, he fell asleep, and did not awake until it was quite day. He arose, and kneeling down in that deserted cabin, he brought all his sorrows before God, and asked in great humility for His guidance and protection.

The storm had passed, and the sun rose in a serene and cloudless sky. After his communion with God, he came out of his retreat to view his surroundings.

The ground was literally covered with pools of standing water, fallen timber and fragments of vegetation. The cabin in which he had slept had been long since deserted, and the place looked mournfully desolate, wild and forsaken.

As the lowlands were now full of standing water, and the creek so high that to return by the way he came was impossible, he took up his satchel and staff, and proceeded westward in search of a settlement.

After wandering on for several hours he came to a large swamp covered with reeds, tall grass and spaces of open water; in some places the covering was a beautiful carpet of green moss, upon which one could stand, but the least movement would shake the frail moss bed for rods around; under this treacherous cover there appeared to be a great depth of quicksand and water. A path made by wild animals along the margin of the swamp somewhat relieved the irksomeness of passing through it.

As he was traveling on he discovered the footprints of a bear which had been turning over some old logs in search of worms and insects. An encounter with Bruin was something for which he was wholly unprepared. Sitting down to consider which course he had better pursue, his attention was attracted by a noise among the bushes behind him. He had already passed the monster and might have escaped unnoticed had he not sat down!

The bear, seeing him, came out of the bushes toward him. As our hero did not show any signs of retreat the bear stopped and sat upon his haunches, ready for a fight. The worn-out missionary did not feel like accepting the challenge, but was rather inclined to a purely defensive policy. The bear remained stationary for some time, waiting, no doubt, for a demonstration of the purposes and ability of the stranger. They eyed each other until that indescribable superiority implanted in the eye of man made the huge beast quail, and he sullenly retreated into the thicket.

The way being now clear our traveler again started on. The marsh was at length passed, but another difficulty now presented itself in the shape of an abrupt bluff; too much fatigued to ascend it, he changed his course by its base, still, however, designing to go westward. A beautiful spring that gushed out from among the rocks at the side of the hill invited him to rest. Whilst laving his sore, feverish feet in its cool waters, he noticed the movements of a little squirrel as it jumped from tree to tree, gathering nuts for the coming winter. Here he learned a lesson which would enable him to appease his hunger.

Having eaten his frugal meal, and being somewhat refreshed, his step was lighter. Another stream impeded his progress, so he again changed his course, following its windings among the valleys and hills. Throughout his whole course he had as yet seen no indications of the presence of man.

The sun was again setting, and as the shades of night increased and no dwelling appeared he began to look about for some place of shelter. As he was hastily ascending a ridge, a pack of wolves commenced their discordant yelps and howlings right in his front. Turning around he wended his way up a ravine, walking as fast as possible. Another pack of wolves then set up a howl to his left; this seemed to enrage the others, so that their hideous noise could not but chill the heart of the defenseless wanderer.

To climb a tree and rest among its branches for the night, was his first thought. A spreading beech, with branches almost reaching the ground, offered its accommodations. After choosing his position in the tree, and fixing himself, as he supposed, for the night, he very soon found his limbs cramped and his hold unsafe. Becoming satisfied that to remain where he was would be risking his life, he immediately descended. The darkness, when off the tree, seemed much more dense; and being now within reach of the wolves, made him almost regret having left it. "Oh, that I never had been called to this sacrifice," involuntarily burst from him. A voice whispered: "The foxes have holes and the birds of the air have nests, but the *Son of Man* hath not where to lay His head." These words were not without effect, for they led him to say, "if the Lord of Lords suffered thus before me, why should I murmer at my lot?" and he again "thanked God and took courage."

At length he succeeded in finding a hollow tree which answered his purpose. Feeling that he was in God's hands, it was not long until "tired nature's sweet restorer" came to his relief.

It is well that God conceals from us the rod with which He intends to chasten us; were it not so, our prospective trials would seem greater than we could bear. The trials encountered by His servant in this peculiar case, were but the beginning of those in store for him.

Having changed his course so often, he lost all idea of the points of the compass. The consequence was that he spent two days and a night longer wandering in this wilderness. At the expiration of that time he found himself at the very old hut in which he had spent the first night; which proved to him that he had been traveling in a circle. Under the circumstances, he was very glad to again avail himself of the protection thus afforded.

CHAPTER III

RELIEF OBTAINED.

THE night having passed, in the morning the missionary felt satisfied that he could not find his way back to the settlement which he had left. For a time he tried to find the old road by which he had come; but failing in this, he directed his steps eastward. His bewilderment having entirely left him, his heart was joyous and his step light. Although the people of the settlement to which he was returning, were comparatively strangers to him, he felt assured that many of them were Christians more than in name, and others who did not bear that name were kind-hearted and charitable. Here was a work for him to do.

The day was rapidly advancing; and the elastic step of the morning had slackened to a laborious effort to reach his destination.

Hark! What sound is that? The tinkling of a bell! He now knew that he was nearing the settlement. Pushing on, he saw to his right several openings, and beyond smoke curling up. He at length reached the gate leading into the yard in front of a farm-house. Everything had a neat and comfortable appearance. That he might here obtain relief, was now his ardent desire.

A dog that lay before the door, observing the stranger at the gate, offered a decided resistance to his entrance. The attention of Mr. Brown, the farmer, was thus attracted, and coming out of the house to see what was the matter, he was struck with the forlorn appearance of the stranger; and with feelings of pity invited him in. The kind look and cordial welcome touched the missionary's heart, and it was with difficulty that he kept back the tears. Taking up his satchel, **Mr. Brown** led the way into the house, and introduced him as "a suffering stranger."

After a few remarks respecting his present situation, he commenced to relate what had befallen him during the past few days. The whole family gathered round to hear his pitiful story; and all were greatly moved by the recital of his sufferings.

"You must now lie down and rest," kindly insisted Mrs. Brown. "I have a comfortable bed prepared for you in the adjoining room. Henry, my boy, will you show the way?"

Henry was a lad about ten years old. A look at his open, honest face at once prepossessed you in his favor. He immediately did what his mother desired.

"Mother," said little blue-eyed Eliza, as soon as the stranger had disappeared, "who is this sick man, and what has he got in his satchel there in the corner?"

"Why, my dear child," replied her mother,

"you should never ask two questions at once. Answering your last question first, I do not know what is in the satchel, nor should my little girl be curious about that which does not concern her. As to the man, he is the missionary who traveled through here last week, trying to get up a Sunday-school in our neighborhood."

"A Sunday-school, mother! School on Sunday! Why he must be a wicked man to keep school on Sunday! I don't want to go."

Her mother never having been in a Sunday-school herself, scarcely knew how to explain to her daughter the difference between it and an ordinary day school. So she simply said:

"It is not a school like ours down at the 'Cross Roads,' but one in which we read the Bible, and sing and pray, and are taught to ove the Saviour."

"O, mother!" exclaimed the child, "then

I would like to go. Do tell the man to have one in our school-house. Will you mother?"

"Yes, child, I will ask him if he gets well again."

"I hope he will get well soon," said Eliza, and bounded off to tell Henry the news. He saw her coming, and as her manner showed that she was greatly pleased, he called out in one breath,

"What have you got? Who gave it to you?"

"I have nothing," she replied; "nobody gave me anything."

"Yes there did," said Henry.

"No there didn't," curtly answered Eliza.

"What tickles you so then," rejoined Henry in a milder tone.

By this time Eliza's ardor was quite dampened by Henry's manner, so she merely replied:

"I will tell you to-morrow," and then left him.

But Henry did not feel like waiting. No

sooner was she gone than he again sought her, more anxious than ever to know what had so excited her.

"I will tell you," she said, "if you wont be so cross to me next time," evidently feeling that she had the advantage of him.

"I wasn't cross. I'll always be good and nice," said Henry, glad to come to terms, for he felt very curious.

Eliza then sat down and told him all that her mother had said about the Sunday-school, occasionally adding an exclamation of her own to make it seem more important.

CHAPTER IV.

AN APPOINTMENT.

MRS. Brown, knowing that the missionary had been deprived of the proper kind of food for such a long time, thought it best that he should now take it in small quantities and at short intervals, and for this reason desired her husband to rouse him, that he might again partake of refreshment. It was now night, and, after a season of devotion, all retired.

The sun had again risen. Hearts had wakened; some to joy and hope, others to sorrow and despair. The missionary had rested well. Although he still looked pale, he had in a great measure recovered from his fatigue. The hospitality of this most excellent family, to whom Providence had directed his steps, was shared with feelings of the deepest gratitude.

Mr. Brown and his wife were earnest, devoted Christians, possessing liberal views, and were ever ready for any movement that could show any reasonable prospect of doing good. They never condemned what had not been faithfully tried, unless forbidden by the Word of God. Although they had never heard a temperance lecture, and, as to a Sunday-school, it was something respecting which their knowledge was very indistinct; yet, when these subjects were laid before them by the missionary, and their great importance shown, both were ready to try the experiment.

"We will make an appointment for you at the school-house as soon as you will be able to fill it," said Mr. Brown, "and then you can explain the whole matter to the people, and we will try what we can do."

"I am ready, with God's help, to commence the work to-morrow," said the missionary.

"Not to-morrow," replied Mr. Brown; "you must not disregard your health when duty does not demand the sacrifice. As this matter has not been much agitated here, and no appointment is out, a few days rest until your strength is sufficient to carry on the work when commenced, will not be a neglect of duty. As the young people have singing-school in our school-house to-morrow afternoon, we will send and have an appointment given out for you on Tuesday evening. We will also have the announcement made at the other school-house; then the people will have a little time to think and talk the matter over, and have their curiosity aroused, and we will have a good turn-out."

"As you seem to understand matters so well, I will leave all to you," said the missionary.

Under the kind care of Mrs. Brown, our

traveler improved rapidly, and his wonted cheerfulness was gradually returning.

"Do you know what is in that bundle there in the corner?" inquired Eliza of her brother Henry, in a loud whisper, and pointing toward the stranger's satchel.

"I guess the stranger has his 'things' in it," answered Henry, looking in the same direction.

The missionary, hearing their conversation, and wishing to gratify their curiosity as well as please them, asked them to bring the satchel to him.

After showing them a book full of pretty pictures and a Sunday-school paper, he allowed them to look at a great many beautiful cards, upon which were printed hymns and prayers. He explained the use of these things, and gave each of them a card and paper. To show "mother" what they had received was of course the next thing to be done, and they had almost forgotten to thank the missionary in their hurry and glee. The mother was almost as much pleased as the children, especially with the papers. After admiring them again, the children asked her to lay them away that they might not become soiled.

Sunday-school scholar, do you prize your cards and papers as these children did? Or do you carelessly soil and lose them—or perhaps tear them up without reading them?

If you have thus indifferently treated them, think of these little children, and, like them, place your Sunday-school gifts among your precious treasures. When you are grown to manhood and womanhood, and called upon to battle with life, you may look upon these mementoes of childhood and youth with sad but sweet recollections.

The next day being Sunday, after the morning duties were finished, this family, with the missionary, enjoyed a season of devotion and Christian fellowship. As they, in the fear of

God, intended to "move upon the enemy's works" on Tuesday night, it would be profitable for the leader to know how the enemy was entrenched, and what forces had been employed against him; how these operated and what their success.

"What kind of people have you here in the West?" inquired the missionary with a smile.

"Well," replied Mr. Brown, "we have what the geographer terms 'a mixed population.' Or, as old Peter Miller would say, 'good, bad and indifferent.' It is a great mistake in eastern men to suppose that the western pioneer is an ignoramus. You will find some of the sharpest, best educated and most energetic men of this continent here in the West. A great many have the 'bump of go-aheadativeness,' as Fowler would say, 'largely developed."

"Method or system is not so much looked upon as 'will it go?' 'will it pay?' 'how long will it take?' The masses are what some term 'fast men.' Money must be made at once! Fortunes acquired in a day! Circuitous approaches are inadmissible. 'Straight through and go ahead' is the cry. 'Young America' here is impatient of delay; and if one way does not at once succeed, another is tried; and if speedy results are not seen, a new location or a change of business is contemplated. Hence, 'fogyism' is generally discarded, and which ever way they move they tend toward the extreme. This restless spirit is the very secret of their being here. Ambitious, brave and independent minds seek their development in situations where they can 'make a country,' create cities, establish commerce, and lay the foundation for learning, art and science."

"Why, indeed, Mr. Brown, you have given me a very graphic description of the characteristics of the western people, and it almost makes me afraid to risk my abilities among such," replied the missionary.

"Never mind," said Mr. Brown, "you must become enthusiastic too; and when they see you are in earnest, they will help you."

"But are there not some 'old fogies' mixed up among the crowd, who would oppose radical measures of any kind?" mildly suggested the missionary.

"Plenty of them," quickly replied Mr. Brown. "It is especially so in religious matters—here they seem to have the most influence, being well-meaning, orderly and good men; but holding the idea that the old routine must be followed, they oppose any change, or any 'new measure,' as they call it; and being men of standing in the community, the result is, in many cases, that nothing is accomplished."

"Are these old measure men inclined to oppose the temperance cause, prayer-meetings, revivals and Sunday-schools by any decided action?" seriously inquired the missionary.

"Some will, and carry others with them, who otherwise might be made active members in the Church; as they are, you cannot tell them from non-professors," rejoined Mr. Brown.

"Are these leading men hard to win over?"

"No, not all," answered Mr. Brown; "they are mostly well-meaning, and if you can convince them of a more effective way, they will go with you; but some are very bigoted."

"What arguments do they generally use against our reformatory movements?" continued the missionary."

"They generally rely upon the supposition that our forefathers lived and died without any of these 'new-fangled doctrines,' and if they went to Heaven without them, we can too."

"Why, don't they see," queried the missionary, "that the Bible is full of temperance, (Acts xxiv. 25; Gal. v. 23; 2 Pet. i. 6; 1

Cor. ix. 25; 1 Titus i. 8); of revivals (Acts ii. 2), and prayer-meetings (Acts i. 13, 14; xvi. 13; xii. 12; Luke xxii. 39–46)? There are also evident commands for teaching the Scriptures to the children, as is done in the Sabbath-school (Gen. xviii. 19; Deut. xxxii. 46; xi. 18, 19; 2 Tim. iii. 15). I do not think they would call these things new, if they would prayerfully study God's Word."

"I wish you would take up these points at the proper time, and give them a full Scriptural illustration," replied Mr. Brown. I think it would be acceptable to the people."

"I will do so; but on Tuesday night I will dwell entirely upon the utility of Sunday-schools."

The hour for singing-school had arrived, and the children had gone, taking with them an "Appointment" written by the missionary, to be handed to the teacher; and they had not forgotten their cards and papers, which they intended to exhibit.

After the singing was over, the teacher read, "God willing, the Sunday-school missionary will deliver a lecture on the subject of Sunday-schools, and, if practicable, organize a school here next Tuesday evening, at early candle-light."

"Who is it?" "What is a Sunday-school like?" were questions asked all around, but were left unanswered. In the meantime, Henry and Eliza's cards and papers had been going the rounds from hand to hand. A general confusion and excitement ensued, ending in a resolve that they must all come on Tuesday night.

The news of the appointment spread like wildfire; the children were excited by the exaggerated descriptions of the cards and papers, and were unanimous in their desire for a Sunday-school.

CHAPTER V.

THE MISSIONARY PREACHES.

ON Tuesday, a beautiful evening closed the day. At an early hour, the parents, together with quite a number of children, also the youth of this and other neighborhoods, were on their way to hear what the stranger had to say; some having made up their minds for, and others against the Sunday-school.

The old school-house was crowded with expectant ones, awaiting the arrival of the "Great Speaker," as he had been reported.

There was a little grove in a ravine behind the barn at Mr. Brown's; this secluded spot the missionary sought before starting to fill his appointment. Here he laid his case before God, asking for preparation of heart, for wisdom, for strength, for words, and, above all, for the power of the Spirit and the ensealing of the truth upon the hearts of his hearers.

Do you wonder that his lecture on that night was endued with power from on high?

Mr. Brown offered to take him to the school-house in his wagon, but as he preferred walking, he went in company with the children, one on each side of him. Their prattling conversation made his heart glad, and he longed to lead all the little ones to the Saviour.

As he entered and took his place at the desk in the school-room, a deep silence pervaded the audience. After offering up a silent prayer, he asked the people to sing a hymn, and all joined in the glorious old tune, "Coronation," with a will. After a short, solemn and impressive prayer, he called the attention of his hearers to the following portion of God's Word: "Therefore shall ye lay up these my words in your heart and in to your soul, and bind them for a sign upon your hand, that they may be as frontlets between your eyes. And ye shall teach them to your children, speaking of them in thine house, and when thou walkest by the way, when thou liest down, and when thou risest up." Deut. xi. 18. 19.

He treated his subject so simply that the children could understand, and with an earnestness that commanded the attention of all. After showing the imperative duty of teaching the Scriptures to our children, and that some *could* not, and others *would* not, thus properly teach them, he said that it was the duty of all Christians to see to it that they were taught. To gather them together on Sunday for religious instruction, was the most appropriate and feasible method. He appealed to the minds and hearts of his audience in such a way as to force their assent to the truth of his propositions; and that, too, from persons who had come with feelings of determined hostility. After another prayer, and the singing of a hymn, he exhibited his Sunday-school books and papers, picture cards and prize tickets, giving to each in turn a proper explanation of its uses, and closed with an appeal to the people to organize a Sunday-school at once.

Upon this, a man arose and said, with considerable faltering, that he objected to any such "snap judgment" being taken; that this Sunday-school fuss was got up by a set of loafers, who were too lazy to work, to swindle their living out of the earnings of honest people. And he, for one, was not going to be led by them. Having thus made known his opinion, he sat down. This man was no other than Mr. Steele, with whom we are already acquainted.

The missionary did not think it prudent to

cast pearls where they would be trampled under foot, so he left the future action to the people.

The short speech of Mr. Steele encouraged those who were prejudiced against any " innovations," and some confusion ensued. Mr Brown arose and said that he was sorry that the gentleman who had just taken his seat had thrown out such unwarranted insinuations; and as he did not offer the slightest evidence to sustain his assertions, he did not feel inclined to give this speech the least credit, and would therefore move that the gentleman, Mr. Steele, be requested to prove the charges made against those who, with the present lecturer, are endeavoring to organize and establish Sunday-schools. This was seconded by three or four, and almost unanimously carried. The time of meeting determined upon was the following Thursday night.

The excitement now became general; there being a division of sentiment among the people, and as this was leading to confusion and impropriety, the meeting was dismissed; but this only gave more liberty, and instead of a calm discussion of the question, extravagant assertions were made, and hasty, inconsiderate conclusions formed, leading to angry words.

A number sought acquaintance with the missionary, and the result of the meeting was that he had warmer friends and more determined enemies than before.

CHAPTER VI.

MR. STEELE'S MEETING.

EARLY on Wednesday morning, the missionary was on his way to canvass the district. He met with opposition and encouragement among the parents, but the children and most of the young people were decidedly in favor of a Sunday-school. His humility and sincerity won him many friends, and before Thursday night came he had disarmed much of the opposition.

The time for Mr. Steele to prove his charges having arrived, the house was filled; indeed many were unable to get in. This, to the missionary, was an omen of good; and he felt calm and strong in faith. The angry scowls of the opposition made no impression upon his feelings, for he well remembered the Saviour had said: "Think not that I am come to send peace on earth ; I came not to send peace, but a sword."

As this was Mr. Steele's meeting, he was on hand. After some delay he arose, and with a great deal of agitation said he reckoned that the time to begin had come, and he guessed he would proceed. He consequently commenced his harangue against the Sabbath-school, and those interested in its success. But being ignorant of the merits of the subject he had undertaken to discuss, he, of course, failed to convince any one. As to his proving his charges, he did not even make the attempt. Even his friends felt that the effort was a total failure, and he sat down without a single expression of applause or commendation from those present.

Some one here asked him what he proposed doing in the matter.

He replied that every one might do as he pleased, but as to himself he would never pay a cent toward the thing, nor ever enter one, nor allow any of his family to be taught in such a shabby concern as a Sunday-school.

A slight effort at cheering, by a few worthless fellows, was made at this boasting declaration, and he felt as though he was of some importance, and took his seat with a smile of complacency.

Mr. Brown was deeply wounded by the uncharitable remarks of Mr. Steele, and he now arose to speak. Every eye was upon him. He commenced by referring to the arguments advanced by the missionary in favor of Sunday-schools; speaking of the positive duty devolving upon all Christians to teach their children the Scriptures, and appealing to the judgment of the whole audience whether any one of the statements made had been refuted by Mr. Steele. He also alluded to the great utility of such an institution, and commented upon the abuse received by persons particularly interested in the cause; he also quoted from Paul, that we should "prove all things, and hold fast that which is good," and not let our prejudices condemn, and our bigotry abuse every one and every thing that is new.

Although there was little expressed sympathy with Mr. Steele and his remarks, it was evident that quite a number could not overcome their prejudices, and stood upon what some termed "neutral ground." Unfortunately for such persons, in morality and religion there can be no neutral ground. Christ says, "He that is not for me is against me."

The missionary now opened his satchel, and taking out a Sunday-school book, laid it upon the table; remarking, that instead of trying to fleece the people out of their money, he would propose to give them fifty volumes like the one before them, if they would make up money to pay for fifty more, and agree to organize a Sunday-school.

The night being now far spent, Mr. Brown proposed to have another meeting on Sunday morning at 10 o'clock, with the object of organizing a Sunday-school. This was agreed to, and the people separated.

A good old Christian, by the name of Law, took the missionary along with him. He was one of those who had long desired a better state of things in the community. The missionary explained to him all that he wished to know, and his already favorable opinions of the Sunday-school were greatly strengthened. From Mr. Law's the missionary went to the next neighbor, who was one of those who professed neutrality in the matter. He appeared to fear the missionary, and did not give him a very warm reception. He said "yes" to everything the missionary said, but was really in doubt as to whether he did not mean "no." Convinced against his will, he hid his convictions by making a doubtful show for the other side. He was left neither cold nor hot; and his hesitating promise that he would come and bring his children to the meeting, was scarcely to be interpreted at all.

Leaving here, the missionary went to Mr. Adams. He was one of the opposition; but he was a frank man, and possessed a superficial knowledge of the Scriptures. He invited the missionary in, intending to "give him a short battle."

After some preliminaries, the objector brought forward his charges, which were about the same as those advanced by Mr. Steele. The missionary answered these one by one, and so plainly showed the utility of the Sunday-school, that Mr. Adams would gladly have escaped from the missionary's presence, and from the conviction forced upon his mind by the truth. His sense of politeness alone prevented him from leaving the house.

As he was a professed Christian, and indeed a leading member of the church, the missionary asked the privilege of praying with the family; this, upon the same principle of courtesy, could not be denied. The missionary had done all that he could in his weakness, and he now laid the case before God; asking for His blessing, His spirit and convincing power. What arguments failed to do, sincere and earnest prayer accomplished.

Sunday-school Agents, Leaders in the Church, Ministers of the Gospel, do you ask God in earnest prayer to bless your labors? Are your efforts made to do good, or to be heard and seen? In the fear of God; in view of the final judgment; examine yourselves in this matter.

CHAPTER VII.

MR. MASON AND MR. WILSON.

ANOTHER clear, calm Sunday morning dawned. All nature seemed to be at rest. The missionary had staid over night with a newly married couple. He found them kind and social, and the young man volunteered his help in the Sunday-school. The hour of ten came, and the school-house was again filled to overflowing. The children were there in full force. God bless the children! What hopes filled their little hearts! Visions of books, papers and pictures floated before their eyes.

The missionary was called upon to conduct the exercises. After singing and prayer, he took as the basis of a few remarks, the words: "Jesus saith to Simon Peter, Simon son of Jonas, 'lovest thou me more than these?' He saith unto Him, 'yea, Lord, thou knowest that I love thee.' He saith unto him, *feed my lambs.*'" What he said was to the point, and disarmed all open opposition. A vote was taken on the question: "Will we now organize a Sunday-school?" This was carried by a handsome majority. When the chairman said: "All who are opposed rise to your feet," Mr. Steele and a few others did so, but the odds against them being so great, they were ashamed, and soon left.

A superintendent was now elected, and happily the choice fell upon Mr. Brown. The subordinate officers were chosen in like manner. A collection was then taken up, which proved to be a liberal one.

The children were formed into classes, and volunteer teachers appointed. A Bible class for adults was also formed, and a short lesson assigned for the following Sunday. The doxology was sung, and the people were dismissed. Thus the good cause seemed to be triumphing over opposition.

A man who lived in an adjoining settlement had come to this meeting, and being favorably impressed with the appearance and manner of the missionary, and the Sunday-school movement, he invited him to pay a visit to the settlement in which he lived, and endeavor to organize a school there.

"I will come," was the laconic reply to the man who gave the invitation. "I will be there by Monday evening."

After obtaining proper directions for finding the place, he took leave of this friend and returned with Mr. Brown. The remainder of the afternoon was employed in giving the superintendent of the newly organized school all needful instructions as to its management, and the best methods of teaching. They both felt happy over the prospects of the enterprise.

Again we find the devoted laborer in the

vineyard of the Lord, acting upon his Master's command. He is now on his way to the neighboring settlement. His journey lay through wood and valley, over hills and prairies—the latter, however, not very extensive. Reaching the settlement, he, in due time, arrived at the house of his friend, where everything had been made ready for his reception. A meal was prepared in a short time, and the missionary partook of it with a decided relish. The long walk and the cordial welcome tended greatly to sharpen his appetite.

The reader will pardon a slight digression. We have followed this servant of God through shadow and sunshine, in his efforts to promote the interests of Christ's kingdom. Let us compare his lot with that of many ministers of the Gospel. Alas! how many are there who, because they cannot possess life's luxuries as well as its comforts, abandon a field in which they might do good! The master has said: "He that taketh not his *cross* and followeth after me, is not worthy of me." Coming back to our missionary, we find him chatting with the children. They were at first rather shy, but his gentle, winning manner soon brought them to his side, and in a very short time they were most excellent friends. In the meantime their father, Mr. Mason, had returned (having been necessarily absent), and welcomed the missionary to his home. As soon as the chores were done, they sat down by a bright fire and entered into conversation. They did not discuss the various topics of the day, nor dissect the characters of their neighbors for the purpose of whiling the time away; but Christ's cause was their theme.

"Are the people here generally in favor of Sunday-schools?" inquired the missionary.

"I do not think they are," frankly answered Mr. Mason. "Few of them care much about anything religious."

"Have you preaching or prayer-meetings?" continued the missionary.

"Sometimes prayer-meetings are started, but they die out directly. Preaching is kept up most of the time by this, that, or the other denomination, but it seems to amount to but little. There is no increase or life about the Church; and you can scarcely tell a member from a non-professor. Indeed, Christianity has fallen into disrepute, and Christ and His cause are brought to an open shame."

"How sad!" replied the missionary, much moved.

"Yes," said Mr. Mason, "it is a great pity; but there seems to be little help for it. Several have *tried* to do something, but all to no purpose. Somehow or other there was no life in it, and Satan, with a few rowdies, defeated every attempt."

"Are all the people so indifferent?" asked the missionary, with great anxiety.

"I do not know that they are; but the exercises were so cold and lifeless that the people had no faith in them; and the conduct of many of the members was so bad, that their influence rather tended to drive men from the Church than lead them to the Saviour."

"What are the morals of the children, as a general thing?"

"Of course, where the church members do not perform their duty, their children are neglected; and when they fail to do right we can hardly expect anything better from worldlings and sinners. Lying, cursing, fighting, disobedience and Sabbath-breaking are common sins among the children. The youth drink, gamble and frolic, and some are guilty of heinous crimes. But, thank God," added Mr. Mason, "there are some noble exceptions both among the children and youth."

"We must pray God to help us to reform this awful state of morals and religion. We must labor and pray until a great revival is brought about in the Church and among the people," said the missionary, earnestly.

"If you talk of a *revival* here they will be

down on you, both in and out of the Church," said the deeply-interested man.

"We will exercise prudence, and call our effort by a more acceptable name; we will call it a *protracted prayer-meeting*," added the missionary, smiling.

"That will be equally obnoxious; the professors generally say, 'we pay the preacher to do the praying for us, and that is enough;' and the irreligious, of course, have little interest in such things."

"What do you think they would say to a temperance meeting?" queried the missionary.

"That will bring down upon you all the loafers, tipplers and rumsellers; indeed nearly all the church members 'take some,' and they would all unite in opposition to you," sadly rejoined Mr. Mason.

"All these things must be overcome. And if we are faithful in using the means God has given us, the work will be accomplished. I do not despair," added the missionary.

"May God help us to do our duty!" said Mr. Mason, as he laid the family Bible on the stand for evening devotion.

CHAPTER VIII.

MISSIONARY VISITS.

THE missionary started on his visiting tour among the people of the settlement on Tuesday morning. The first house to which he came indicated a good share of worldly comfort. He met the owner repairing the garden-gate, and accosted him with, "Good morning." The man looked at him as if hesitating whether or not to reply, and said, "How d'ye do." The missionary, still undaunted, made some remarks of a commonplace nature, which were answered in monosyllables. As the missionary felt that he had no time to waste, he came at once to the subject of his mission.

"So you're the fellow getting up Sunday-schools. I thought you were by your looks; but let me tell you at once that 'you're barking up the wrong tree here,' and the sooner you 'play quits' the better. I have no time to fool away in talking about such nonsense."

"But pray tell what objections you can have to teaching the young the Holy Scriptures?" mildly interposed the missionary.

"I just now told you that I had no time to waste in talking to idlers, and I expect you to take the hint,' sharply retorted the unreasonable man.

Finding that there was no chance at present to do anything with him, the missionary bid him "Good-day," and started. The man replied with a triumphant "Good-bye, sir," at the same time casting toward him a sneering look.

As the missionary was passing the barn, he met a little girl, to whom he gave a card for herself and another for the family.

On crossing a little stream he met a young lady on horseback; to her he handed a tract, entitled, "Are you Saved?" A slight tremor was visible when she read this; the question demanded an answer. Seeing how the title affected her, he prayed God to bless the words to her salvation.

He did not go far until he came to a place where two roads crossed at right angles; so he sat down a moment to rest and consider which road to take. Whilst sitting, a man with a wagon and a fine span of horses came along. His countenance bespoke a kind heart, and the missionary rose to salute him. He responded with a hearty " Good-day," and an invitation to take a ride, if the stranger were going his way. The missionary had to confess that he did not know where he was going, and unfolded his object in visiting the settlement.

The man said that he had heard of a Sunday-school being organized at Clear Creek, but he was not up when the meeting was held, and knew but little of the nature of the institution. Still he would be willing to " give the thing a trial," if it did not *cost too much.*

" As to the cost," said the missionary, "that will depend upon the number of books, papers, maps and other helps you get. But I will agree to donate to your school, if you establish one, half of a good library."

This opened the eyes of the man to their utmost extent, and he exclaimed:

"Why, you don't say! That don't look like speculating or swindling people out of their money, as they say of you around here. I never did believe the half I heard; it didn't seem reasonable to me. But," continued he, " I don't believe that we can make it go. Everybody I have talked to is down on it."

" Would you be willing to assist me, and bring your family long enough to test the matter?" inquired the missionary

"I'll do my best, if things are as you say. I believe the children ought to be instructed in the Bible the moment they are capable of understanding it."

"Are there any others that you think would join us in the work?"

The stranger, Mr. Wilson, hesitated, and then said; "People here seem to be dead in regard to anything of this kind. Whether we succeed or not, a general fight over the question will, if it can possibly stir them up, be of some use. Make the appointment, and I'll stir them out."

"When shall it be?" inquired the missionary.

"Put it on Friday night; there is spelling-school in our school-house to-morrow night, and I'll go down and have it given out, and the whole neighborhood will know it," said Mr. Wilson, with great animation.

"Providence permitting, I will be there," said the missionary.

"And give us a speech, telling all about the Sunday-school," suggested Mr. Wilson.

As the missionary was about to offer his hand and say good-bye, Mr. Wilson said:

"Won't you go with me and stay until Friday? I can accommodate you."

"I thank you, but I will not visit the neighborhood until Friday, and then I will come to your house and we will go to the meeting together," replied the missionary.

"Well, perhaps that will be best," rejoined Mr. Wilson, and passed on. Calling back, he said: "Take the road up the hill; it will lead you through the most thickly settled portion of this neighborhood." The missionary nodded his head and took the road as directed. He met with various successes in his itinerancy until Thursday evening, when he was shamefully treated by a man known as 'Squire Hunt, one of the leading men of the settlement. The missionary bore the insults meekly, but upheld the cause of Christ manfully.

CHAPTER IX.

OPPOSITION.

ACCORDING to promise, the missionary was at Mr. Wilson's house, and he, together with the family, went to the schoolhouse. The words of his text were, "Train up a child in the way he should go, and when he is old he will not depart from it." Prov. xxii. 6. He approached his subject with caution, for the people before him were restless and excited; but he gradually unfolded the solemn truth contained in the text. He addressed himself to the parents, especially to the mothers. His apparent sincerity and great earnestness overcame the prejudices of many, but still a large majority were opposed, or cared little about the matter.

The 'Squire got up and denounced the speaker, Sunday-schools and Temperance societies. He was frequently cheered; and those who had been won by the earnest eloquence of the speaker, were now carried away by the majority, and were inclined to "follow the multitude to do evil." The 'Squire then called upon the people to decide by a vote, whether they would have a Sunday-school or not, shouting out: "All who are in favor of a Sunday-school here, rise to your feet." Mr. Wilson and Mr. Mason sprang to their feet like heroes, their intrepidity encouraging some of the timid and wavering, who, together with their children, made quite a respectable vote. After these were again seated, all who were opposed to a Sunday-school were called upon to rise. Instantly several of the most bitter opposers, who were waiting for the word, were up; others. soon followed, while the 'Squire was urging the fearful and lukewarm with, "Up! up! I know you are opposed; show your colors!" and in this way succeeded in getting many to rise, who did not really intend to have anything to do with the matter. He then declared the majority opposed, and in triumph took his seat.

Mr. Mason arose and asked the majority to concede to those who desired it the privilege of holding Sunday-school in the school-house undisturbed.

This very reasonable request was opposed by the 'Squire; but upon the vote being taken, the privilege was granted. This was something gained, and the missionary was thankful for it, although he and his little band were openly subjected to sneers and abuse. But they had the comforting assurance that "all things work together for good to them that love God."

On Saturday morning, the missionary started for Clear Creek Settlement. On his way he met a little boy and two little girls.

"How do you do, my young friends?" kindly began the missionary.

They all smiled pleasantly, but did not say anything.

"How old are you, my son?" continued he, addressing the boy.

"Ten, next Christmas; my birthday comes day before Christmas," ingenuously answered the boy.

"These little girls are your sisters, I suppose?"

"Yes, sir," responded the boy.

"Can you read?"

"Yes, sir, I can read in the 'Introduction,' very well; my sister Jane can read too; and little Betty can spell and read easy words," answered the boy, with some feelings of pride.

"Did you ever go to Sunday-school?" inquired the missionary.

"*No, sir!*" answered the boy, emphatically "We don't go to school on Sundays; we go on week-days." This direct answer caused the missionary to smile; he continued, however, with the question, "Would you like to, if there were a Sunday-school?"

"No, sir!" again replied the boy. "We play ball, pitch horse-shoes, or go a fishing on Sunday, and I like that better than going to school."

"Don't you think it is wrong to do such things on Sunday?"

"No, sir," again responded the boy, "father and all the neighbors do that on Sunday."

The parents then were the examples; and the children followed. How many parents thus unwittingly take their children by the hand and lead them down to death!

"You all go to meeting sometimes, don't you?" continued the missionary.

"Yes, sir, once in a while."

"Don't the preacher talk against such things?"

"Sometimes; but nobody cares. Some go

to the grocery and pitch horse-shoes for whisky; and some go to the tavern to play checkers or such, for a dram, or for fun," replied the boy.

"Don't the preacher talk against drinking liquor and lying about at the grocery on Sundays?" seriously inquired the missionary.

"No, sir, *he likes it himself.*"

"It is a bad thing to drink whisky," said the missionary.

"Yes, sir," quickly responded the boy; "last night they had a spree at the grocery, and Bill Jones liken'd to've killed Tom Miller with his knife; and Ace Ross knocked Old Butt's eye out. Father says they have a law suit to-day."

"What a pity!" said the missionary, shaking his head. "Do you live far from here?"

"About a mile," answered the boy.

The missionary then gave each of the children a card, and explained to them, as far as they were capable of understanding, what a Sunday-school was like; and they then said that they would like to go to such a school. He told them of an appointment for Sunday afternoon at 3 o'clock, in the school-house near Mr. Wilson's, and invited them to come and bring their parents along; he then said " Good-bye," and left them.

Having detained himself longer than he supposed, he was compelled to hurry on, as he had quite a distance to go before he would reach Mr. Brown's. As he was passing through a lane, after coming within the bounds of Clear Creek Settlement, he found two men lying in a fence-corner, drunk! He tried to rouse them, but failed in so doing, for they were past consciousness. Continuing on, he soon came to the grocery. Happily for the missionary, the crowd within was all excitement over a " drinking game ;" that is, several engaged in playing cards for a treat of the whole company. Before he had passed out of hearing, a great shout and uproar at this den of sin, told him that the game was up, and the treat was being given. In his heart he then resolved that a Temperance society should be established in that place, and he prayed God to help him in the undertaking. After arriving at Mr. Brown's, he could not but compare the revolting scenes he had left behind him, with the pleasant, social intercourse he was now enjoying.

CHAPTER X.

SUNDAY-SCHOOL ORGANIZED—LOCAL PREACHER.

AT the appointed time, on the Holy morning, the missionary and Mr. Brown were in the Sunday-school, ready for action. A number had already collected, and after the opening exercises, the missionary delivered a short and impressive address, in which he exhorted the teachers to aim at the conversion of those placed under their instruction, to be always punctual, to set a godly example, and, finally, not to grow weary in well-doing, but continue the work through evil as well as good report; and reminded them of the reward on the final day of reckoning.

Everything passed off well; the children

were pleased, and the parents greatly encouraged. The opposition could see nothing to condemn, but Mr. Steele and a few others laughed at the " simple thing," and hooted at the idea of sending their children.

According to arrangement, Mr. Mason came with his horses and wagon for the purpose of taking the missionary to the other settlement. It had been announced to the people that an effort to organize a Sunday-school would be made on the afternoon of this day. By 3 o'clock many had come together; some for the purpose of taking part in the enterprise, and others merely to look on. The school was started, though under less auspicious circumstances than the one at Clear Creek; yet it was a beginning. The result was in God's hands.

During the week that followed, the missionary visited the families of the settlement, urging the parents either to take or send their children to the Sunday-school. His kindness and persuasive address won him more friends than promises. The force of public opinion against the school made many fear to take part in it; the most of the people, however, began to treat him with respect.

On Thursday evening he again preached. He was prepared for the occasion, not by a written sermon with rounded paragraphs and beautifully-finished sentences, but by constant, fervent prayer, and thoughtful meditation. He had contemplated the state of the people, and the weight of immortal souls lay heavily upon his heart; and, above all, he remembered his commission and his great responsibility, for the Almighty had said: "If the watchman see the sword come and blow not the trumpet, and the people are not warned; if the sword come and take any person from among them, he is taken away in his iniquity; but his blood will I require at the watchman's hand."

The opponents found that they had an earnest man to contend with; a man with the whole armor on, and one who could wield the "sword of the spirit" with power; that he was not only "mighty in the Scriptures," but "full of the Holy Ghost;" and they saw that if they did not immediately "do something," he would be "master of the situation."

So they went to work, as is usual in such cases, to misrepresent his language and misconstrue his meaning; to change the truth into falsehood, by adding, distorting and detracting. His character, too, was assailed, and scandalous stories invented and circulated in order to ruin him; but he heeded them not; for the Saviour had said: "Blessed are ye when men shall revile you and persecute you, and say all manner of evil against you falsely for my sake; rejoice and be exceeding glad, for great is your reward in Heaven."

Whilst the missionary was still in this neighborhood, he was called to the bedside of a dying woman. Now that the hour of dissolution was rapidly approaching, she began to have misgivings about her fitness for Heaven. She had been in the Church for a number of years, but was not a lively stone in the building. After conversation and prayer with the missionary, her faith was strengthened, and she felt ready to go at the Master's call. Thus did this servant of God do good upon every possible occasion. Having learned that a local preacher, who lived a few miles distant, was opposed to Sunday-schools, he determined to call upon him and talk over the matter.

The missionary, upon reaching the home of the preacher, found him ready to start out to fill an appointment at a place about six miles distant. He treated the missionary coldly, and boastingly told him that he and his people had gotten along for many years without Sunday-schools, and he guessed they were as good as those who had them, and reckoned they could still make out without his services; and to tell those who sent him "to attend to their own business and let other people's alone." Not waiting for a reply, the preacher gave his horse a cut with the whip, and was off. There was consequently no alternative left the missionary but to retrace his steps. This he did, and attended to the duties set apart for the day.

Notwithstanding opposition, the work went on; and the friends of the Sunday-school became daily more respected by its enemies.

CHAPTER XI.

MR. KERR AND HIS FAMILY.

UPON one occasion, as the missionary was passing through the western portion of Clear Creek Settlement, he called at a house whose surroundings seemed familiar. The man of the house, too, appeared to him as one he had seen before, but he could not remember exactly where.

After some general remarks, he said to the man, "I almost fancy that I have seen you before to-day."

"I suppose you have," the man replied, with considerable agitation; and continued, "Do you not remember some time ago, standing at a gate and requesting a farmer to allow you to stay all night, and being refused, and that there was another man there beside the owner of the place?"

The missionary said he did.

And you remember, also, that you gave a little boy and girl some picture-cards and tracts?"

"I do," said the missionary.

"And one for each of the men at the barn?"

"Yes, I well remember that."

"I was that man," said he, somewhat confused, "and when Mr. Steele refused to let you stay, I, like a coward, approved of it. Don't you remember?"

"Yes, I believe you did," gently replied the missionary.

"Yes, I did that very wicked thing, and now ask your pardon. I have had no rest since, on account of it," said the man with emotion.

"I have long since forgiven you," calmly

replied the missionary. "Such things do not move me; I count them as nothing."

"If you had suffered what I did from them, you would count them a good deal. I heard you preach last Sunday, and if I had not been ashamed, I would have made a public confession of my wickedness. I thank God that you have come this way," continued the humbled man with faltering voice, and stretching out his hand for reconciliation and forgiveness.

Joyfully the servant of Christ gave Mr. Kerr (whom our readers must have recognized) his hand, and their friendship was sealed.

Mrs. Kerr, who had been absent at the time of the missionary's arrival, now came in. She recognized him at once, and welcomed him with unfeigned kindness.

"Where in the world have you been since you were here last month?" inquired the free-spoken woman. "I wondered and wondered," she continued, "what had become of you in the big storm. I expected nothing else than to hear that you got killed in that dreadful rain. It was awful! I declare I thought our house would go!"

"Oh," pleasantly replied the missionary, "I put up without 'leave or license,' at a hut out on Walnut Creek, where I was taken care of."

"Why, nobody lives out there that I know of," said Mr. Kerr. "Let me see; was it about due west from where you left us?"

"Very nearly, I think," said the missionary, at the same time smiling.

"Well, sir, I know of but one family that ever lived in that swampy, sickly, mosquito hole, and two or three of them died there and the rest moved away long ago," replied Mr. Kerr, instantly adding, "What is the man's name that lives there?"

"Indeed I cannot give the name," answered the missionary, with such a look of mischief that Mrs. Kerr declared that he was only joking. "It was at the place you mention, no doubt, that I staid. There were two graves on a hill near the house, which was in a very dilapidated condition, and the yard was overgrown with weeds and briars; indeed, everything presented the appearance of having been long deserted."

"That was Mr. Kelly's home once, but the mosquitoes and chills drove him out. It was well he left, or the whole family would soon have perished there. It is a poor country compared with this," explained Mr. Kerr.

"But you said that you were well taken care of; I'd like to know who took care of you," said Mrs. Kerr, with a mischievous twinkle in her eyes.

"The Lord took care of me," he replied.

"Oh, yes, I did not think of that;" said she. "Did you keep dry in the old hut in that dreadful storm?" she added; and in the same breath continued, "Didn't you think the whole thing would blow down over your head?"

"I was pretty well sheltered from the wind and rain, but I really did think more than once that all would go down."

"I was sure our house was gone," earnestly resumed Mrs. Kerr, "and I expected nothing else than the death of all of us."

"When we are ready," he replied, "death is no evil."

This practical reply rather embarrassed her, and for a moment she was at a loss to know what to say next; so he continued:

"To crush the body is a matter of little consequence; but the soul, the immortal being that inhabits this house of clay, is of immense value. Could we fully realize the fact that nothing dies but the clay we inhabit, we would not dread the change."

Mrs. Kerr listened attentively, but made no reply.

"Will you be so kind as to give us an

account of your troubles on that dreadful night?" asked Mr. Kerr.

"Certainly," said he, and he related to them the long list of trials, dangers and privations through which he had passed.

Tears more than once filled the eyes of the eager listeners. "And now," said Mr. Kerr, after the missionary had finished, "I must give you some of my experience since we parted. If you remember one of the cards you gave the children, read, 'And these shall go away into everlasting punishment, but the righteous into life eternal;' *that* fell into my hands. When I read those words the irresistible conviction struck me that *I* would be one of '*these,*' and a fearful looking for judgment to come took hold of me. All the way home I seemed to hear the words, 'And these shall go away into everlasting punishment.' I wished again and again that I had only taken you with me; or at least have defended you against the unreasonableness of Mr. Steele.

But that was now too late, and I groaned under the lashes of my guilty conscience. Upon reaching home, my wife told me that you had been here and prayed with the family. I suffered greatly, and was at length compelled to 'own up' to my wife, who soon discovered that all was not right with me—and she strongly condemned my action." Mr. Kerr did not cease speaking until he had made a full confession of the humiliation he had experienced from a guilty conscience.

The missionary could not but be moved at the penitent recital; yet he rejoiced that Mr. Kerr was at last led to the true and only source of comfort.

After uniting in prayer with the family, the missionary inquired if they had been to the Sunday-school.

"Oh yes," heartily replied Mr. Kerr, "we were all over last Sunday, and had a delightful time."

"No doubt; indeed, no one with proper

feelings, and a regard for the eternal interests of his children or the children of others, can help being benefited and highly delighted in a well-ordered Sunday-school," said the good man with emphasis; adding, "have the books and papers for which they sent, come?"

"They have," rejoined Mr. Kerr, and I verily thought the whole school would go wild when the box was opened. Indeed, I was myself considerably excited; and when each one received a book and a paper, I really could not refrain from shedding tears, in witnessing the uncontrollable delight that filled every heart; and I reproached myself with bitterness for having been so cowardly as not to defend this noble institution, when you and it were assailed by Mr. Steele. To-day, I thank God for the Sunday-school! and I know that every family that attends it thanks God for it."

"May God, the Divine Author of this institution, foster and bless it to the salvation of all who attend it, or are within its holy influence!" said the delighted missionary; adding, "how is that gentleman who was with you at the gate getting along?"

"Oh, pretty well; but he doesn't take any stock in Sunday-schools—he is very angry at me for attending, and won't speak to me."

"We must pray God to give us grace to bear with him, and try to gain him to our confidence," said the missionary.

The day was passing, and the good man would have gone on, but Mr. Kerr and his wife would not hear to it, insisting that he should remain, at least over night; so he consented to remain until morning.

By the side of the looking-glass, in the room which he occupied, he found hanging a framed card, containing the text, "And these shall go away into everlasting punishment, but the righteous into life eternal." Underneath was written in a plain hand, "Saved by grace, through this little card. James Kerr."

Here was a secret. Mr. Kerr attributed his conversion to the teaching of this silent monitor. What a momentous result can hang upon an insignificant cause! It is said, that "the obstruction of a straw at the fountain-head, may change the channel of a mighty river." Never should we despise the day of small things.

CHAPTER XII.

THE TEMPERANCE CAUSE.

THE missionary, after bidding farewell to the kind friends with whom he had spent the night, again went on his way, "Seeking the lost sheep of the house of Israel." He had not gone far before he met two children, who proved to be Mr. Steele's. Upon entering into conversation with them, he found that they remembered him. Their bright, intelligent answers to his questions, led him to regret more deeply that they were kept from the influence of the Sunday-school. The innate kindness of heart manifested by these children made him feel that, if properly trained, they would become useful members of society and the church; so, with a view to using all possible influence in their favor, we again find him an unwelcome visitor on the farm of Mr. Steele.

The farmer was at the time unloading wood, and scarcely noticed the missionary; the latter soon broached the subject occupying his thoughts, by saying,

"My friend, could you not consent to take your children to Sunday-school once, on trial?"

"*No sir!*" he roared; "and I don't want you to bother me any more about it;" and continued, "work like I do, and let your betters alone."

"Well then," said the missionary, "if you will not go yourself, will you not permit your children to go? I know that the school would be a great benefit to them, and"——

"I don't want to hear any more of your nonsense—just 'git,' you lazy loafer," retorted the angry man.

The missionary having failed to accomplish the object of his visit, left with feelings of sadness; he went on his way, however, doing with his might whatsoever his hand found to do, and he had the pleasure of seeing the schools increasing in numbers and influence. This increase was secured only by hard work —the various difficulties attending all movements aiming at changing fixed customs had to be overcome. One by one, these *were* overcome; and although many opposed the work, and others were indifferent and careless, most of the best men and women of the settlements were in favor of the schools. Nor were they afraid to give their money in support of the good cause, nor unwilling to sacrifice ease and pleasure, if necessary; for they well knew that even in this world they would receive tenfold reward, and in the world to come, everlasting life.

Parents, come with your children to the Sunday-school; it is the nursery of the Lord, in which plants are reared for the garden of Heaven—the Paradise of God!

Young man, wend your way to the Bible-class, and thereby shun the temptation of the Sabbath-breaker and the snares of the transgressor! And you, young woman, blooming in all the loveliness of life's early dream, shun the society of those who mock at religion, and the teachings of the Holy Word, and fly for your life to the place where prayer is wont to be made—where the better qualities of your nature will be fostered, and your heart taught to love the Saviour!

The missionary felt that the time had now come for him to attempt to establish a Temperance Society among these people for whom he had been laboring. This was a hazardous undertaking, where the habits of the people were so firmly fixed in favor of using intoxicating liquors as a common beverage. But a meeting for that purpose was appointed and the whole country was aroused. Those favoring the cause, though few in number, were willing to take the responsibility, and the missionary promised to do his best; he was aware that those of the opposition were powerful, having on their side *appetite, self-interest, custom* and *public opinion;* but he was not in the least dismayed; he knew in whom he had believed; and although the gates of Hell should oppose, yet they could not prevail.

The time for the meeting having arrived, after singing a hymn and offering a prayer, the missionary called the attention of his large audience to the following words:

"Who hath woe? who hath sorrow? who hath contention? who hath babbling? who hath wounds without cause? who hath redness of eyes? They that tarry long at the wine! They that go to seek mixed wine! Look not thou upon the wine when it is red, when it giveth its color in the cup, when it moveth itself aright; at last it biteth like a serpent and stingeth like an adder!" Prov. xxiii. 29–32.

He then demonstrated by example and facts, the truth of the answer given to these questions. Taking up the last part of his subject in the words, "At last it biteth," &c., he gave a most fearful description of the effects of spirituous liquors upon the human system and the immortal soul—depicting with great force the awful condition of the poor rum-enslaved, soul-degraded drunkard, both in body and mind. He held up to their gaze the emaciated form of a heart-broken wife, and the half-famished images of her little ones.

He also stated that intoxicating liquors were the parent of every conceivable sin, and had extended the catalogue of crimes until language could scarcely furnish a name for the atrocious iniquities—that they filled the jails and poor-houses, at the expense of the industrious and good, and also furnished subjects for the gibbet.

He alluded also to the groceries, declaring them the prolific schools in which the young were taught the rudiments of sin, in idleness, vulgarity, profanity and drinking—thus preparing the way for infamy and crime, and daily training the mind for the service of Satan.

He then enforced the command in the text, not even to look upon it—saying that the apostle had commanded to "Abstain from all *appearance* of evil."

He also declared that there was no neutral ground between virtue and vice—between supporting and opposing this source of evil; that we must be either for or against it.

He concluded with an appeal to the people to save themselves and those around them from the fangs of the serpent and the sting of the adder, and to organize at once an army to fight unto death this monster, Intemperance.

A pledge was written and laid upon the

desk; after it was read and a few words of explanation given, all who wished to join the society were requested to rise and give their names. Quite a number of men, women and children instantly responded to the call; among them were several tipplers and two hardened drunkards, whilst the moralist and the moderate drinker refused to aid in the work of reformation. There can be no doubt that these persons were "stumbling-blocks in the way of sinners;" and the position taken by them sealed the fate of more than one poor soul. And there were also elders and deacons, class-leaders and gray-headed Christians, unwilling to deny themselves of the "lusts of the flesh," but went with the "customs and maxims of the world"—taking their morning dram, their favorite bitters, and with themselves, training their families in the way leading to drunkenness and death!

After the people had been dismissed, those who had given their names signed the pledge with their own hands, and organized a society, by electing officers and framing a constitution for the government and permanent efficiency of the same. Upwards of sixty put their names to the "Declaration of Independence" of the tyrant, "King Alcohol!"

This was a glorious beginning—and the wives and children of those tipplers and drunkards who joined, shed tears of joy, and their hearts overflowed with thankfulness to God and His messenger.

CHAPTER XIII.

THE MISSIONARY'S DEPARTURE.

THE missionary was loth to depart from this interesting field of labor, but he was called, and must obey. He "threw his mantle" upon the shoulders of a noble young man, whose name was Truman; he was a fluent speaker, and an enthusiast in whatever he believed to be right; a giant in courage and bodily strength, and above all, a conscientious Christian; to him was consigned the care of this noble enterprise.

The rum-sellers, with their dupes, were now aroused to a full sense of the power arrayed against them; they justified their conduct, by holding up that of the ministers and leading men in the Church, and the latter would quote Paul's advice to Timothy, where he says, "Drink no longer water, but use a little wine for thy stomach's sake, and thine often infirmities." Tim. v. 23.

"Here," they boastingly said, "wine is commanded as a drink;" and dared a refutation.

But Truman showed them that this passage did not only *not* prove that wine should be used as a common drink, but *proved* that it should only be used as a medicine. He showed them, too, that Paul was a Temperance Lecturer, and not afraid to reprove rulers before whom he "reasoned of righteousness, *temperance*, and judgment to come."

The argument that Christ *turned water into wine* was also brought forward; the reply to this was, that there was no evidence that the miraculous transformation contained a single particle of intoxicating matter; whilst every rational supposition, based upon the holy character and pure doctrines of the Redeemer, would most emphatically declare that there was not.

Such was the acute and powerful reasoning of this young man, that minister and deacon were silenced, if not convinced. Mr. Truman having been himself snatched from the very vortex of ruin, his experience in the dens of infamy, and knowledge of the workings of the whole traffic, enabled him to bring the truth home to the hearts of his hearers in a very effective manner.

As the faithful missionary could delay no longer, he appointed the time to preach his farewell sermons in the two settlements. The first meeting was to be held in the Clear Creek school-house immediately after Sunday-school. The day was pleasant and the school well attended; the exercises of the same having been completed, order was called, that all might have the benefit of the missionary's parting advice. He made a short address, and then desired each child to come to him, that he might shake hands and bestow a trifling gift by which he might be remembered. He would live in the memories of all, however, without anything of this kind. A half hour after the dismissal of the Sunday-school, the people had assembled to hear the "farewell sermon." The text was, "And now, brethren, I commend you to God and to the word of His grace, which is able to build you up, and give you an inheritance among all them which are sanctified." Acts xx. 32. The sermon which followed was adapted, in every respect, to the occasion.

As all earthly ties must sooner or later be sundered, this shepherd and his flock were compelled to part. It is needless to say that the separation was sorrowful on both sides.

After leaving Clear Creek Settlement, the missionary filled his appointment at the other place; and the parting which took place here, was but a repetition of the first one.

We now find him on his way to a work among strangers in a strange land: he knew what would probably befall him, but he had counted the cost, and, like Paul, was willing to endure hardships as a good soldier.

Here, for the present, we will leave this noble, earnest and devout Christian.

CHAPTER XIV.

WORKING OF THE SABBATH-SCHOOL AND TEMPERANCE SOCIETY.

IT will now be our purpose to follow some of the results of the missionary's labors among these people. In our present narrative we can notice but comparatively few incidents among the many interesting ones that transpired, and bring before our reader but few of the characters connected with the development of the various plans.

In addition to there being two Sunday-schools and one Temperance Society firmly established, the Christian Church under various names was most effectually aroused—many of its members being abundantly blest and their spiritual strength renewed; backsliders were reclaimed, and sinners awakened and converted: there were also prayer-meetings held in the different houses among the people.

A general contest, however, was kept up between those opposed to these institutions, and their defenders. As soon as it was generally known that the missionary had left, the rum-sellers and their adherents became bold in their opposition; they appeared to think that, if the shepherd had gone, the sheep would be scattered. Even some of the ministers would not come out boldly on the side of this reformation.

Well did Isaiah prophesy, "For the leaders of this people cause them to err; and they that are led of them are destroyed. Therefore the Lord shall have no joy in their young men, neither have mercy on their fatherless and widows: for every one is a hypocrite, and an evil doer, and every mouth speaketh folly.

The Temperance Cause met with the most

opposition; and some who stood faithfully by the Sunday-school could not give up old habits; although they did not particularly oppose the Cause, their support was weak and doubtful. Those who took no interest in the Sunday-school were decidedly against temperance. Thus the people became more and more divided—and the stinging truths of Mr. Truman seemed to set everything on fire; and the Saviour's prediction respecting a house being divided against itself, seemed to be literally fulfilled. Every demonstration of truth was met with increased hostility; and, like Herod and Pilate, even enemies were made friends in condemning Christ. This, however, only drove the faithful few nearer to the Rock of Ages, which was their "stronghold in the day of trouble;" it made them "search the Scriptures" more, and more vigilant in prayer; relying upon God for help. Hence they maintained their ground, and in time were able to make inroads into the enemy's country, taking captives and plucking brands from the eternal burnings. Those of the opposition, in order to fully carry out their principles, were driven to indorse and defend the lowest morality, and the coldest and most formal type of Christianity—and were compelled to yield to the caprices of the ungodly by excusing their faults.

In order more fully to impress the truth upon the heart, we will now give a brief narrative of the characters and lives of two families—representatives of the parties formed through the labors of the missionary. The circumstances bringing him to our notice, also introduce us to the family of Mr. Steele —the other family is that of Mr. Brown, of the same neighborhood. Through the former will be illustrated the effects of opposing religious training as carried on in the Sunday-school; and through the latter will be shown the inestimable blessings resulting from such training, and the value of vital godliness.

Mr. Steele, as we are already aware, had two children, George and Mary—also a wife, who was naturally a most excellent person; but the influence of her cold-hearted husband was not without its effect upon her life. He claimed to be a church member, but he had only a "name to live." After years of constant association with such a person, we need not wonder that she quietly submitted to him.

Mr. Brown and family, also consisting of a wife and two children, had always been on terms of intimacy with Mr. Steele's family. On Saturday afternoon, previous to the opening of the Sunday-school at Clear Creek Settlement, George and Mary Steele went to Mr. Brown's on an errand, and received permission to spend an hour with their friends, Henry and Eliza; the Sunday-school was the all-absorbing topic of conversation, and although George and Mary knew that their father was opposed to anything of the kind, they still hoped that they would be allowed to go on the following day. No sooner had they reached home, than they began to tell their mother, in a very excited manner, about the Sunday-school. Just as their excitement was about at its height, their father entered the room, and in a very gruff manner asked, what "all this fuss" was about. As the song of the robin ceases at the crack of the rifle, so suddenly ceased the story and the joy of these children. They looked to their mother for help; she had no hope of a patient hearing, so she merely said:

"The children were telling about the Sunday-school, and"——

"Sunday-school! yes, they were over there at Brown's, and have had their heads filled with nonsense—have they?"

The mother's lips were sealed. The humility and silence that greeted him only vexed him the more; so, seeing no opposition offered, he commenced again on the aggressive. Addressing his wife in tones of haughty reproach, he said:

"I'd like to know whether you and these little brats are going to side with every whining loafer that comes about?"

Then turning to the children, who were crying, he said:

"I'd like to know what you are bawling about? If you don't soon shut up you'll wish you had."

The children again looked at their mother; but as she was still silent, George stammered out, "We want to go to Sunday-school, father."

Little Mary, with her eyes sparkling in tears, now ventured with,

"Do, father, let us go—won't you, father?"

This was said with such a beseeching voice and hopeful look, that for the instant the storm was lulled; and had the mother joined her children in their petition, perhaps a limited privilege might have been obtained for them. But she failed! The precious moment went by unimproved, and all was lost!

The father would not listen to what his better feelings suggested; so he told the children decidedly that they should not go to the Sunday-school, and if they did not stop crying he would punish them severely. After he left the house, their mother endeavored to console them; but they felt that they had been unjustly treated, and wished to know *why* they could not go to Sunday-school. Their mother did not attempt to give the reason; for she, too, felt that they had been wronged.

Supper-time came, but the children's grief had taken their appetite, so their mother excused them from coming to the table. Their father, finding that they were not coming, and knowing the reason, whipped them severely and forced them to come; they sat down and tried to eat, but every mouthful seemed to choke them. The mother's eyes were dim with tears, and the meal was eaten in silence. The father's face was flushed, and he hurried through his supper, being anxious to get away from the presence of those whom he had wronged. When he had gone out, the mother again tried to soothe the children, but their father's absence only gave them the liberty to sob aloud; their mother, fearing that he might return and hear them, bade them go out to the barn and hunt the eggs, and be good children.

"We want to go to Sunday-school and learn to be good," said they. Every word of this went straight to the heart of the mother. The children went and did what their mother had desired; as they staid out longer than she thought necessary, she became troubled and started in search of them. Hearing George's voice, she listened and found that he was praying, and Mary was repeating the words after him. A consciousness of having failed in the performance of her duty filled her heart with anguish, and she went into the barn and joined them in prayer; but her faith was weak—she feared her husband more than God. She resolved, however, to make the attempt to plead in behalf of the children; going into the house, she found her husband trying to find something to interest him in an old newspaper. Her heart beat between hope and fear; taking a seat she commenced her petition.

"Is your head turned too?" he sneeringly asked. "I guess, the next thing I know, you'll have an agency and the pretty loafer lounging around here. But let him come," he continued; "just let soap-stick come; I'll kick him out of my house so quick, that he won't know what hurt him."

The wife's heart was too full for utterance, so she said nothing. Construing her silence into contempt, he resumed fiercely.

"*You've* been poking this stuff into the

children's heads yourself, have you? I'll beat it out of them, mind you!" said he, shaking his fist in the air. The mother's resolution was gone, and she meekly replied, "No, I have not said anything." She yielded all for the sake of appeasing her husband. After berating the missionary and making some threats about "this fuss in the family," Mr. Steele went to bed.

Had this father but consented to "prove all things," as the apostle had recommended, all of the unhappiness now existing in his family might have been avoided.

CHAPTER XV.

GEORGE AND MARY

THE Sunday-school having been successfully organized, Mr. Steele was extremely vexed, and he withdrew himself as far as possible from those who went with the missionary in the movement. He was, besides, ambitious and proud—he could not bear to think that "a traveling loafer," as he termed the missionary, should overcome him; and, being considered the champion of the opposition, he mingled with the wicked, courting their praise, and bringing himself to their level. He was fighting in vain, for it was against God.

A few more weeks passed away, and it

having been quite a while since George and Mary had seen their friends, they asked their mother if they might make Henry and Eliza a visit; she referred them to their father for permission. George persuaded Mary to ask, for he knew that his little sister's winning manner would be more likely to accomplish the object; watching her opportunity, she climbed upon her father's knee, and putting her arms around his neck, kissed him; she had done so before, but not for some time. The caress pleased him, and he returned the kiss. Not thinking of anything in particular, he said, "Well, what else do you want, my little pet?"

"You wouldn't give me what I wanted, anyhow, would you father?"

"Certainly, anything you ask;" and he gave her another kiss, adding, "Well, pet, what is it?"

"George and I would *so* much like to go see Henry and Eliza—may we?"

For a moment he was in doubt, the nature of the request being so unexpected; but for once he allowed his better nature to have sway, and consented on condition that they would come home early. They were soon on their way, as happy as the birds on a sunny morning.

Henry and Eliza were delighted to see them, and entertained them by giving a minute account of all that transpired in the Sunday-school; they also gave them some of the cards and papers which they had received there.

George and Mary kept their promise to "come home early." Whilst they were showing their mother the Sunday-school cards and papers, their father entered the room. He became very angry upon being thus reminded of the subject so disagreeable to him; so, seizing the children's gifts, he tore them into pieces and then threw them out the window, and declared that the children should never go to Mr. Brown's again. The result of such a course on his part, was that the hearts of his children were hardened against him; they felt that they had been unkindly and unjustly treated, and they very soon became irritable and peevish in disposition. Their father soon discovered the change, and knowing the cause, he determined to restore them to their usual spirits by affording them amusement; so he induced them to seek new playmates, among those who did not attend Sunday-school. They obeyed; but, at first, such company was exceedingly disagreeable to them, for the children with whom they associated were profane and vulgar and did not regard God's Holy day. They had been taught by their mother that such conduct was wrong; but the father now ruled with a rod of iron, and all were compelled to bend to his will.

The downward course is rapid; it was but a few short years before George and Mary, surrounded by such influence, could mock with the mocker, at the prayer-meeting and Sunday-school.

The father, annoyed by the success of the good cause, and a consciousness of wrong-doing, sought relief in drink—hence he was thrown into the society of the worthless, vulgar drunkards, who lie around the haunts of vice. Insensibly, he was drifting down to irretrievable ruin!

He never expected to be a drunkard—not he! No, he could drink when he pleased, and let it alone when he pleased. He would show "that crazy Truman," that a man could *govern* his appetite, and that he did not speak the truth when he said that confirmed whisky-drinkers would fill drunkards' graves.

He found out to his own sorrow who spoke the truth; for the time came when he was compelled to give up his comfortable home to satisfy the tavern-keeper's demands. His wife, through disappointment and abuse, lost her health and died broken-hearted, before her husband and children had run their whole course of sin.

CHAPTER XVI.

MR. BROWN'S FAMILY—MR. STEELE.

WHILST the Steele family was descending deeper and deeper into sin and degradation, the family of Mr. Brown was advancing in virtue, honor and holiness. Henry and Eliza were faithful members of Christ's visible Church—they had been taught to love the Saviour in the Sunday-school; they were now teachers in the same, and by their love and practical instructions, their humble piety and fervent prayers, they led more than one to the Fountain of Life.

Henry, like his father, was a noble-looking man, of very prepossessing appearance. His taste for the beautiful and true increased with his years, and his knowledge of many subjects became extensive and thorough—thus was he fitted for almost any position of honor and trust.

Eliza's naturally amiable disposition was developed to advantage under Christian influence, and she married a man whose high moral and religious excellence made him eminently worthy of her. Living in anticipation of joys to come, she could not help being happy.

Passing over a few more years, we will look, for a time, at the little Mary of other days. In a forlorn old hut, far away from any other house, we find her crouched upon the floor, shivering with the cold, and in almost a starving condition; her father had left her some weeks previous, under the pretence that he was going in search of work; her brother had long since gone from the place, with little or no purpose in view; she knew nothing of his whereabouts, and it seemed to her that she was now utterly forsaken, for she had received no word from her father during his absence. She wished that she might die—not thinking or caring what the consequence would be. As she sat thus, musing over her sad lot, Providence seemed to direct the steps of Mr. Brown, whose business called him to that part of the country, to the old hut; his heart was touched at the sight of her sufferings, and it was not long before he made arrangements for her removal to his own house; and he and his wife exerted themselves to win this wandering child to the straight and narrow path. Although it took a long time for her to break up her old habits, she at length became a follower of the meek and lowly Jesus. Mr. and Mrs. Brown were father and mother to her, and she endeavored in every possible way to show her gratitude for kindness so freely bestowed.

Time passed on, and Mary, not hearing

anything of her father, grieved for him as dead; although she never knew to any certainty that such was the case.

On a clear, cold morning, about a year after Mr. Steele had left his daughter, as a party of hunters were crossing a prairie many miles distant from Clear Creek Settlement, they found the body of a man who had evidently been frozen to death. Any one could see at a glance that he had been a drinking character, and most probably under the influence of liquor at the time of his death. The hunters took the body to the nearest settlement, and made inquiry as to who it might be; none knew excepting a grocer, who came forward and stated that this man had chopped wood for him on the day previous, and, according to his own request, took his pay in whisky; after this no one remembered having seen him, but it was supposed by those present at this time, that he had become intoxicated, and after wandering on for some time, had fallen down in a drunken stupor, from which he never awoke in this world. Whether or not the grocer, who had been an actor in this tragedy, had any compunctions of conscience at this time, we are unable to say; he interested himself, however, in procuring a rough box in which the remains of Mr. Steele (for it was he), were placed, and buried by those who never had known him in life. Thus ended the career of one who depended upon his own strength to resist temptation, and set himself up in opposition to the means employed for the furtherance of God's cause. This may be an extreme case, but it is not the first instance in which God has visited retribution in this world.

CHAPTER XVII.

THE MISSIONARY AGAIN VISITS THE WEST.

IN that beautiful season of the year in which the missionary first visited the West, he was again on his way thither, but not with his pilgrim-staff—that was now laid aside. He could no longer travel hundreds of miles on foot as he once did—he was now in a carriage with the venerable Mr. Mason.

He had written to his people in the West, promising to visit them if they would send a conveyance for him, as he was no longer able to walk, and was too poor to go by stage. Yes, he was poor in this world's goods, but rich in Christ—an heir of Heaven!

No sooner was his letter received, than it

was read in the churches and Sunday-schools, and a liberal collection was soon taken up, to insure every convenience necessary for his accommodation; and Mr. Mason volunteered to bring him out. The journey proved to be a great advantage to his failing health.

The appearance of things was very much changed to him, for eighteen years had elapsed since he first came to this place. The little ones had grown up, the youth were heads of families, and the locks of the older persons were turning gray, and many had gone the way of all the earth. Many new settlers had come in, the little hut villages had become towns, the trails and wood-paths were now highways and stage-routes, the log school-houses had become substantial frame churches, and the wilderness in which the missionary had suffered was now being settled and covered with new farms. His friends in the cause of Christ, Mr. Brown and Mr. Wilson and Mr. Truman, the defender of Temperance, were still alive, "Steadfast and unmovable, always abounding in the work of the Lord."

Many blessed seasons he enjoyed with them, and they were often "sitting in heavenly places in Christ Jesus." After a rest of some days, the missionary felt able to preach and lecture among the people. The opposition to Sunday-schools and the cause of Temperance had in a great measure subsided; public opinion, that great leveler of uprisings, had taken sides with the "new measures," for the very elements of the Western character demand progress and life. The missionary's preaching was especially blest to the Sunday-schools; through his efforts whole classes, with their teachers, were brought into the Church.

During one of these gracious seasons, when many were turning to the Lord, a dreadful murder was committed at one of the groceries in the village. One of the Sunday-school teachers, and a noted advocate of Temperance, heard that one of his class had been persuaded to accompany a man to a grocery. The teacher resolved to save his scholar from the influence of the fiends who were aiming at his destruction; he succeeded in getting the boy to leave the place. They had taken but a few steps, when some one rushed up behind the young man, and stabbed him in the back under the shoulder blade, piercing his heart. The knife did its work effectually, for he expired in almost a moment's time.

The excitement following this event was intense. There were several persons present, who held the murdered young man in high esteem; these arrested the murderer and held him secure. In the meantime, the news of the atrocious deed spread all over the country, and hundreds gathered to the scene of blood. Had it not been for the high state of religious interest prevailing, lynch law would have been executed upon the heartless criminal, by hanging him to the nearest tree; but an officer was allowed to lead him away to a place of confinement.

The young man's body was conveyed to his father's house amid weeping and lamentations. This was too much for some of the people; and, as if actuated by a sense of justice, they went back and demolished the den as a common nuisance. All the liquors were destroyed and the owners prosecuted. This was summary work; but the general temperament of the Western people is such, that they not unfrequently take the law into their own hands, when they fear that justice will be tardy or uncertain from the courts.

On the day appointed for the funeral of the young man, hundreds were early at the house of the dead. The Temperance Societies were all present in mourning. Many who, through his instrumentality, had been led to Christ were there, and shed tears of genuine grief over his remains; aged Christians groaned in their sorrow. Indeed, there was scarcely one present who was not moved to tears.

The missionary preached the funeral sermon from John xi, 25 :—"I am the resurrection and the life; he that believeth in me, though he were dead, yet shall he live." He alluded to the consolation afforded in the sentence referring to eternal life. He exhorted all to prepare for death, and dealt the rumsellers a blow, which, connected with the circumstances that brought them together, led them to think, at least, of what they were doing. He concluded with a reference to the exemplary Christian character of the deceased, and exhorted all to follow him, as far as he had followed Christ.

Several other ministers were present, who also delivered short addresses of a very impressive character. These were followed by Mr. Truman, who made one of the most eloquent and masterly appeals in behalf of the Temperance cause ever made in that country. An aged minister then led in prayer, after which the painful exercises were closed.

CHAPTER XVIII.

DEATH.

THE murderer had been taken to the county jail to await his trial. In the meantime, suspicion was aroused that the prisoner was George Steele, but he steadily denied it, and insisted that he was John Pogue. The rumor coming to Mary's ears, she at once feared that it might be true; and to relieve her mind of the dreadful suspense, she resolved to know the worst, and hence obtained permission to enter his cell. When the door was opened, there, in chains, sat George! Although she had felt that it would be so, she was nevertheless shocked at the sight before her. He tried to evade the recognition, but his heart failed; ungovernable emotions unmanned him, and he wept like a child.

"George, my brother, my dear brother, how could you do that thing?" she exclaimed, and her whole frame shook as she spoke. After a while she became more calm and asked the keeper to allow her to be alone with her brother for a short time; he consented, and she sat down on the bed, close beside her brother, as she did years ago, when they played under the elm-tree at their dear old home. He told her all—"But," said he, " I was in liquor, and a fiend seemed to drive me to the awful deed! I was not to blame so much; I did not use to be so, did I, Mary?"

"No, George," she gently replied, "you were once a good boy;" and then, after hesitating a moment, she said, " do you pray now, brother?"

He looked at her in a dreamy way, and

said, "*I* pray! I cannot pray!" then his eye kindled, and he continued, "*I* am not to blame; when you and I wanted to be good father would not let us, but taught us that Sabbath-breaking, swearing, dancing and drinking were only amusements that everybody should enjoy; and we soon learned to like these things, Mary—and where am I now?" She leaned her head upon her hands and sighed; then rousing herself, said hopefully, "It is not too late yet, George; God has been merciful to me, and has pardoned all my sins; if you repent as I did, He will not cast you off; but you must pray, George, with all your heart."

Looking into her eyes, he replied by saying, "*You* pray for me, Mary." Kneeling down, she brought her poor, sinful brother's case before the Mercy-seat; but there was no godly sorrow for sin in his heart—the fear of death made him wish for prayers. Had he been at liberty, he would have been as bad as ever; and no wonder pardon was not granted. After Mary rose from her knees, she had some further conversation with her brother, and then took leave of him with a heavy heart. This was their last meeting. The time for George's trial arrived; the court-room was crowded with curious and idle spectators; the prisoner was brought forward to answer the charge of murder; he pleaded "Not guilty." A plea of insanity was set up by his counsel, and an artful defense made for him; but the case was clear, and the testimony against him overwhelming.

The Judge of the district was Henry Brown. The prisoner was directed to stand up; the Judge asked him if he had anything further to say, why sentence of death should not be pronounced; he shook his head and faltered, "*No.*" After receiving his sentence, he desired to see the Judge. They met. Neither could speak—a convulsive pressure of hands was all that passed between them.

What a contrast is here! Both men occupied the same social position in childhood; yet a difference in training and associations brought about the present result. May God help us to take warning!

Thirty days were given the prisoner to prepare for the eternal future. His jailer was kind to him, and offered to get him any religious advice he desired; at first he refused to see any one, but as the time of death drew nearer, he consented; the missionary to whom he had given a cup of water in his boyhood was ready and anxious to go to him; and no sooner had he received George's permission, than he was at his side, endeavoring to shed light upon his darkened understanding; but the good man's prayers and advice seemed to produce little or no impression upon the mind and heart of George. He felt that there was no hope for him, and as the missionary left him he requested him to preach his funeral sermon, and in doing so, warn others not to follow the example of one whose earthly career was short, and ended in death and everlasting misery.

We will now draw a veil over the closing scene in the life of this young man. In doing so, we would say to the Sunday-school scholar, bear in mind your great privileges—do not abuse them—do not consider it a task, but a pleasure, to prepare the lessons given you— keep ever before your mind the fact, that it is your soul's eternal interest, and God's glory, for which you must work.

The missionary lived several years after his return to his Eastern home; and, like Paul, he would frequently write an epistle to his brethren in the West—thus could their hearts still commune with each other. But the time came when this laborer in the Master's vineyard was called to rest. The close of his life was as calm as the summer evening upon which he was called. With the apostle he could say, "I have fought a good fight, I have finished my course, I have kept the faith. Henceforth there is laid up for me a crown of righteousness, which the Lord, the righteous Judge, shall give at that day—and not to me only, but unto all them that love His appearing."

Compare the death of the earnest, working Christian, with that of the opposer of truth or of the cold-hearted formalist. After death comes the judgment!—and the Saviour has said, that the former shall live and reign with Him, whilst the latter shall go away into everlasting punishment.

Reader, to which of these classes do *you* belong?

THE END.

www.ingramcontent.com/pod-product-compliance
Lightning Source LLC
Chambersburg PA
CBHW030340170426
43202CB00010B/1184